"THE THING THAT IS ESSENTIAL TO BECOMING AN ARTIST, SOMETHING KIDS DO AND ARTISTS KEEP ON DOING AFTER THEY GROW UP, IS PLAY." —VIK MUNIZ

JELLY, GARBAGE + TOYS

MAKING PICTURES
with VIK MUNIZ

Vik Muniz

in collaboration with

Joan Sommers, Amanda Freymann, and Ascha Drake

Abrams Books for Young Readers

New York

I GREW UP POOR, BUT I'VE BEEN PRETTY LUCKY.

Me, at age 3, in São Paulo, Brazil

My earliest memories are sitting in a chair with my grandma and a book. She taught me how to read, but in a different way than most kids learn. My grandma never went to school, so she taught me to memorize the shape of each word. I didn't learn the alphabet, and I struggled to read and write in school, so I turned to another language—**DRAWING.**

I DREW ALL THE TIME in school. One day my math teacher sent me to the principal's office with my notebooks, which were full of my illustrations. I expected to be punished, but instead I was asked to enter an art contest. I won the contest and was awarded a scholarship to an art academy for drawing and sculpture, which I went to after school for three years.

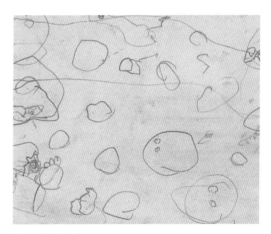

My earliest drawing

I was able to get to the United States because of a bullet—I was shot in the leg after I broke up a fight. It turned out that the guy who shot me was rich, and he paid me not to take him to court. I used the money to buy a plane ticket to Chicago, and from there I moved to New York City.

In America I had many jobs before I was able to make my living as an artist—I was a waiter, a bouncer, a grocery store bagger; I worked at a roller rink and at a gas station. And I was constantly **LOOKING AT ART**—visiting museums and going to galleries.

Five years after coming to the United States, I had my first gallery show. The works I exhibited were objects I called "relics"—like this one, titled *Clown Skull*, a funny remnant from a very evolved race of entertainers.

When the gallery hired a professional to photograph these relics, my interest in the medium of **PHOTOGRAPHY** was ignited. I realized I could photograph my artwork from a certain angle, adjust the light and focus, and create an image that matched the one in my head—my original idea for the work. By taking a photograph I can **CONTROL HOW THE VIEWER "SEES" MY ART.**

Clown Skull, from the series *Relics*, 1989

People always ask me, "When did you become an artist?" I always answer that I don't remember when I became an artist, but I do remember when everybody around me stopped being an artist. **YOU ARE ALL ARTISTS.** You are born with a unique way of looking at things that is different from grown-ups.

The thing that is essential to becoming an artist, something you guys do and artists keep doing even after they grow up, is **PLAY.** When you play, you **TRY STUFF OUT,** see what works. If something doesn't work, it doesn't matter because you're just playing, right? It's just for fun. You have to play in order to learn.

Have you ever watched people in a museum or gallery? I do, all the time. They back away from an artwork to see the whole image and figure out the story, then they get right up close to see the paint, or whatever the artwork is made of. That dance between the **IDEA OF THE ART** and the **MATERIALS** used, the moment when the one turns into the other, is **MAGICAL.**

Tupperware Sarcophage, 2010

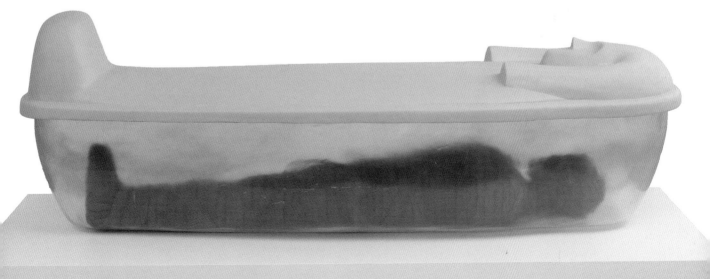

THE WORLD IS MY ART SUPPLY STORE.

WHAT DO I USE TO MAKE MY ART? As you'll see in this book, I use everything—cotton, thread, wire, sugar, chocolate, peanut butter, jelly, plastic toys, magazines, dust, trash, puzzle pieces . . . even liver cells!

I "draw" or "paint" with these materials to make an image, which I then photograph. I destroy the original so I can reuse the materials. So I'm really a **PHOTOGRAPHER.** I want my photographs to remind adults of the way they used to see things when they were kids like you.

One of the ideas I play with is **RECOGNITION.**

Everybody has seen things in clouds, right? You look at a cloud, and it looks like a plane or it looks like a dragon . . . but you have to already know what a plane or a dragon looks like, or you wouldn't recognize it.

Rower, from the series *Equivalents*, 1993

WHAT DO YOU SEE HERE?

  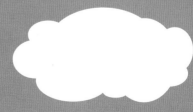

What if you make an object that looks like a cloud, and a lump of cotton, and a guy rowing a kayak? And check this out . . . the moment you see the guy rowing the kayak, you forget the lump of cotton and you forget the cloud. The moment you think the object is a cloud, you can't see the guy rowing the kayak.

We can have only **ONE THOUGHT AT A TIME.** This is because we have something called "attention." Attention is both a help, because it keeps you focused, and a handicap, because you can think about only one thing at a time. At least YOU can decide what you want to focus on in a picture—so you can see the cloud, or the guy rowing, or the lump of cotton.

Here's another. Do you see a cloud, a kitty, or a piece of cotton?

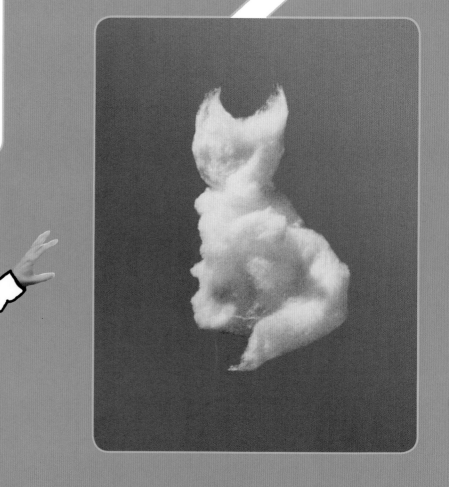

Kitty Cloud, from the series *Equivalents*, 1993

DRAWING DOESN'T LOOK LIKE MAGIC, BUT IT IS.

I'LL SHOW YOU!
Make a circle like this . . .

then add radiating lines . . .

and you have . . .

 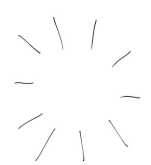 

something quite magical. I brought the **SUN**, an immense ball of fire eight light-minutes from Earth, to this page with one simple drawing. It's magic because I made you **THINK** about it.

I started making pictures that, when you see them from a distance, make you say, "Oh, they're just pencil drawings," but when you look more closely, you say, **"HEY, WAIT A MINUTE!"**

These aren't drawings—they're **PHOTOGRAPHS OF WIRE:** a tied-up bundle, a lightbulb, clothes drying on a line, and a monkey holding a camera!

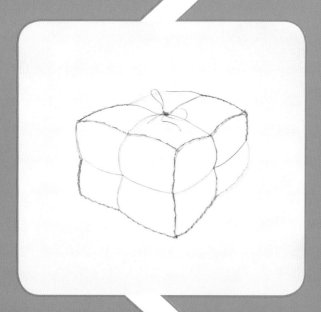

Then you start **REALLY THINKING,** and before you know it, you're not just looking at art. Instead, you're thinking about the **WAY** you're **LOOKING** at it, and this is very important.

Top, left to right: *Parcel, Fiat Lux.* Bottom: *Brooklyn Scene,* all from the series *Pictures of Wire,* 1995. Opposite: *Homage to Darwin (aka Monkey with Leica)* (detail) from the series *Pictures of Wire,* 1995

I DON'T WANT PEOPLE TO SIMPLY SEE A REPRESENTATION OF SOMETHING. I WANT THEM TO SEE *HOW* IT COMES ABOUT.

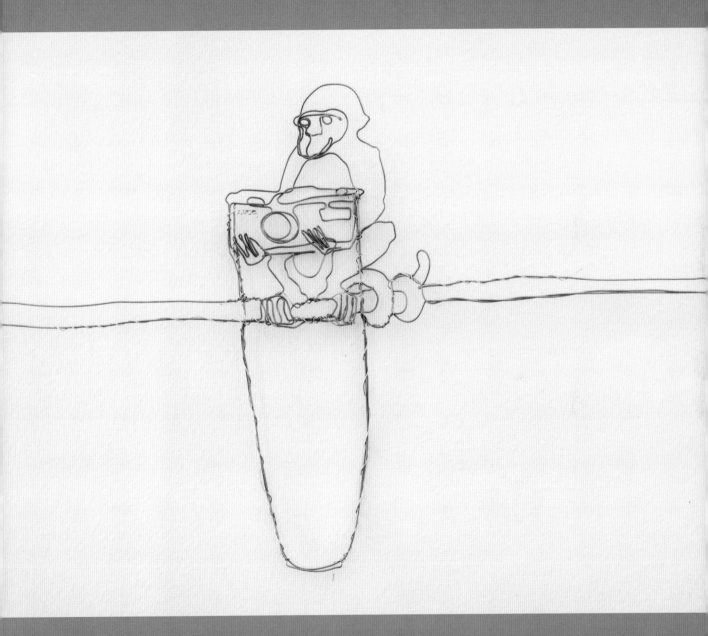

MAKING DETAILED DRAWINGS WITH WIRE IS VERY DIFFICULT, SO I THOUGHT, "WHAT ABOUT THREAD?"

Using thread allows me to play with images that have **PERSPECTIVE,** or depth. This one is my version of a print by Corot called *The Dreamer.*

It's of a man looking over a valley, but at the same time it's just thread piled up on a surface. Again, you can choose what to see: the man and the trees or just the thread.

As a kid, I loved to fly kites, and we bought kite thread by the yard. Four hundred yards of thread would send my kite over the mountains, so far that we couldn't see it. Look where you can go with 16,000 yards!

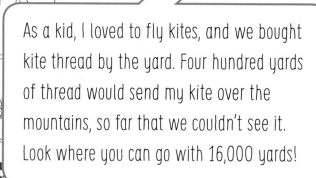

16,000 Yards (Le Songeur, after Corot), from the series *Pictures of Thread,* 1996

AFTER MAKING PICTURES WITH LINES, I THOUGHT MAYBE I COULD MAKE PICTURES USING LITTLE GRAINS.

I went to an island in the Caribbean called Saint Kitts, and I spent two weeks just **PLAYING** with some kids I met. They were the sweetest kids.

SAINT KITTS

NEVIS

I got to know their names and a little about each of them. Even though they lived on an island surrounded by water, they had never learned to swim. They circled around me in the water, and I would hold them up and help them swim.

My last day on the island, the kids invited me to meet their parents. Unlike their children, the parents were very sad and tired. I wondered, "How do these children become those grown-ups?"

I soon found out. The parents worked sixteen hours a day cutting sugarcane on plantations. It was very, very hard work. When they came home, they had no energy, nothing left to give.

So I thought I would make portraits of these kids out of sugar because of the sweetness that was taken from them to make them into very bitter adults.

Opposite: *Valentina, the Fastest,* from the series *Sugar Children,* 1996

When I returned home, I re-created the photos I had taken of the kids by sprinkling white sugar onto black paper using little sifters, and then I took photographs of these sugar "drawings."

Drawing with sugar is easier than drawing with a pencil because you don't have to erase—you just lick your finger and **EAT ANY MISTAKES!**

After I finished each portrait, I put the sugar in a little glass jar and glued the child's photograph on it as a label.

I showed the portraits at a small gallery in New York, and the *New York Times* wrote a nice review, and then I was invited to be in a major exhibition.

Now these portraits hang in some of the best museums in the world and in the library of the kids' school. It's important that everybody is able to see art.

IT'S AMAZING. THESE KIDS ARE THE REASON I BECAME FAMOUS—I OWE EVERYTHING TO THEM.

Opposite: *Ten Ten's Weed Necklace*, from the series *Sugar Children*, 1996. Above: Picture jars containing the sugar used in *Sugar Children*, 1996

Wait a minute . . . the **TASTE** of the material adds another layer of meaning. If I told you that the sugar portraits were made of salt or snow, you would see them differently— right? So what if I draw with something that has a very complex taste?

LIKE CHOCOLATE! Chocolate is complex because it is made from cacao beans, which are very bitter. Cacao does not taste good. But adding sugar makes it delicious. And people think of so many different things when they think of chocolate. I decided to paint with chocolate syrup. Chocolate syrup dries very quickly and becomes dull, so I had about an hour to finish each painting.

This picture, made of chocolate syrup, is based on a famous photograph of Jackson Pollock creating one of his "action paintings." Pollock often laid his canvas on the floor and dripped or splashed paint on it. My painting is very small, but I photographed it with a big camera and made **HUGE PRINTS.**

These chocolate pictures are so big that when you see one in a gallery or museum, you have to **BACK UP** to see the whole thing, then **GET CLOSE** to see that it's made of chocolate.

Opposite: *Action Photo III (after Hans Namuth)* from the series *Pictures of Chocolate*, 1997
© Vik Muniz and the Estate of Hans Namuth/VAGA, NY

After sugar and chocolate, I wanted to make pictures using every **FOOD** in the kitchen.

I created a double *Mona Lisa*, after Da Vinci's iconic portrait, out of peanut butter and jelly!

I made *Medusa Marinara*, my version of a famous painting by Caravaggio, using spaghetti and tomato sauce!

I HAVE USED SPICES LIKE CURRY, CHILI POWDER, AND BLACK PEPPER—AND EVEN SMELLY FISH EGGS—TO MAKE PICTURES.

Opposite: *Individuals* (detail), from the series *Pictures of Chocolate*, 1998. Top: *Double Mona Lisa* (*Peanut Butter + Jelly*), from the series *After Warhol*, 1999; bottom: *Medusa Marinara*, 1999; under flap: Caravaggio, *Medusa*, c. 1596–98

And then I thought, instead of using food, I can make drawings with **THINGS!** Here is an artwork I made using little toy soldiers. It's actually a sad picture—it's a portrait of a kid who, at fourteen years old, was going off to fight in the American Civil War. He was a soldier at an age when he should have been playing with toys.

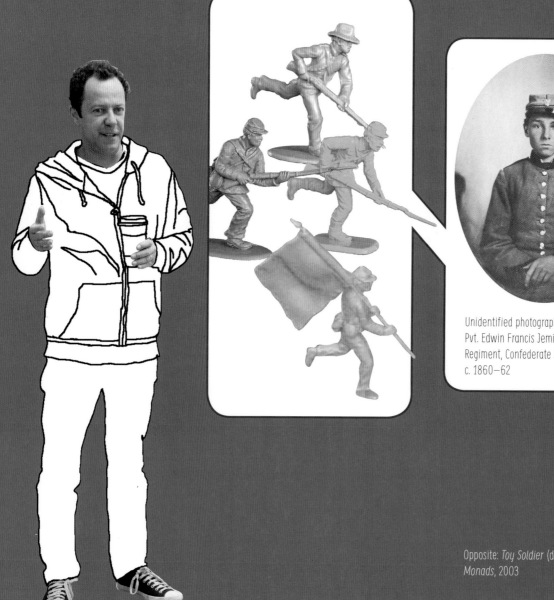

Unidentified photographer, portrait of Pvt. Edwin Francis Jemison, 2nd Louisiana Regiment, Confederate States of America, c. 1860–62

Opposite: *Toy Soldier* (detail), from the series *Monads*, 2003

I do a lot of self-portraits because if they turn out ugly, nobody gets mad. This is me with a terrible headache. It's made of thousands of little **TOYS.**

I have boxes and boxes of toys in my studio, and my team and I just make the pictures on the floor. Notice that this self-portrait is photographed from an angle. The camera is not positioned directly above. Because of that, you see the toys in **PERSPECTIVE.**

There are Pokémon dolls and Creepy Crawlers—toys that you probably have at home. I even signed my portrait using toys! Can you find my name?

Self Portrait (I Am Too Sad to Tell You, after Bas Jan Ader), from the series *Rebus*, 2003

I WAS KIND OF A COWARD WHEN IT CAME TO WORKING WITH COLOR.

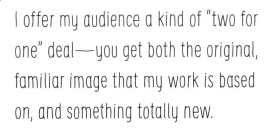

I offer my audience a kind of "two for one" deal—you get both the original, familiar image that my work is based on, and something totally new.

My old, low-resolution computer monitor gave me an idea. You've seen **PIXELATED IMAGES,** right? I used thousands of Pantone color chips arranged in a grid to re-create artworks like Chuck Close's self-portrait or Mark Rothko's abstract painting. I photographed each work when it was finished. The *Pictures of Color* look like pixelated digital images, but it's also easy to see the material they're made of—colored paper squares.

After Mark Rothko, from the series *Pictures of Color*, 2001

Opposite: *Chuck*, from the series *Pictures of Color*, 2001

I ALWAYS WANT TO HOLD THE VIEWER IN FRONT OF AN ARTWORK A LITTLE LONGER.

I never went to art museums as a kid. Brazil didn't have many! Until I went to the art academy, my exposure to art was old picture books with faded colors. I remember the first time I saw a beautiful book on Impressionism! I was struck by the work of Monet and Cézanne.

To create these images I used a paper punch to make colored confetti out of old magazines and books.

I photographed the collages and then enlarged them, so each confetti-like dot became the size of a silver dollar.

Irises after Van Gogh, from the series *Pictures of Magazines*, 2004

Opposite: *Still Life with Apples after Cézanne*, from the series *Pictures of Magazines*, 2004. Under flap: Paul Cézanne, *Still Life with Apples*, c. 1890

I wanted to use the **EARTH** as a **CANVAS.** I was inspired by Robert Smithson, an artist who made "land sculptures." His most famous work, *Spiral Jetty*, is a massive winding road built in the Great Salt Lake in Utah. I've never seen the real thing, only photos of it. First I made a model of *Spiral Jetty* in my studio.

PHOTOGRAPHY LETS YOU LIE AND TELL THE TRUTH AT THE SAME TIME.

But I needed to work **BIG** and I wanted to play with real tractors (I'm such a kid), so I convinced a Brazilian mining company to help me. I mapped out my drawings using GPS and then had huge trucks and bulldozers carve them in the dirt. An envelope, dice, scissors, a hanger, an electrical outlet—dumb stuff! Then I went up in a helicopter to photograph them.

I MADE HUGE DRAWINGS OF REALLY SILLY THINGS!

We made thirty *Earthworks*, some as long as a half mile (1 km). You can still see some of them from an airplane or by using Google Earth. Maybe far in the future, some aliens will look at them and say, "That civilization was so weird!"

While I had massive trucks digging away in Brazil, I was also making a series of miniature *Earthworks* in my studio. These "fakes" are made out of sand, and are only about 16 inches (40 cm) long.

I used the same camera to shoot both the small and the enormous *Earthworks* and I printed all the photographs at the same size.

Opposite: *Brooklyn, New York (Spiral Jetty, after Robert Smithson), 1979.*
Above: *Scissors* (detail), from the series *Earthworks*, 2002

CAN YOU TELL WHICH *EARTHWORKS* ARE "REAL" AND WHICH ARE "FAKE"?

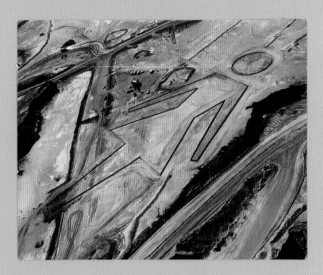

I like to mix photographs of the real ones with photographs of the fake ones when they hang in an exhibition.

Can you find clues in the photographs that tell you about the **SCALE?**

Opposite: *Outlet (Fabrica, Iron Mine)* (detail), from the series *Earthworks*, 2005

MAYBE YOU'VE BUILT SAND
CASTLES AT THE BEACH.

For four years I collaborated with scientists at MIT to figure out how to draw a castle . . . on a **GRAIN OF SAND!** We used an electron microscope with a focused ion beam (FIB) to etch superfine lines on grains of sand so small they were invisible to the eye. The etchings were then scanned and printed very large.

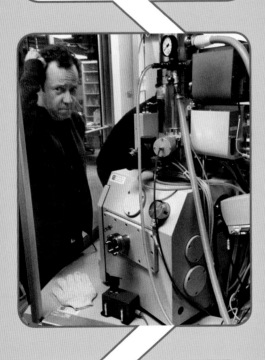

I'm scratching my head because I had no idea how to make that FIB machine work!

I'VE MADE HUGE PHOTOGRAPHS OF TINY THINGS, AND TINY PHOTOGRAPHS OF HUGE THINGS!

Opposite: *Sandcastle #3* (detail), from the series *Sandcastles*, 2013. Top: *Sandcastle #1*, from the series *Sandcastles*, 2013. Bottom: *Sandcastle #10*, from the series *Sandcastles*, 2014

CAN BEING INVOLVED IN MAKING ART CHANGE PEOPLE'S LIVES?

Until 2012 the world's largest garbage dump was in Jardim Gramacho, a small town just outside Rio de Janeiro. It was where everything that is not good ended up. I spent three years with the "catadores," or pickers, who worked there. They sorted through mountains of trash, barely making a living by scavenging metal, collecting plastic, and unearthing treasures that could be recycled or sold.

Each picker has a story—of a lost child, of suffering from an addiction or an abusive husband, or of a serious illness—some bad luck that brought them to Jardim Gramacho. They recycled trash to keep their families fed. As Suellen, a young catadora, pointed out, "We are working honestly—we're earning our living."

I wanted to prove to myself that art was important, that it could change people's lives. So I chose to work with the pickers—who had never been to a museum or a gallery, who knew nothing about art—to make **IMAGES USING GARBAGE,** the material they dealt with every day (which is some very ugly material).

WHAT HAPPENED WAS AMAZING . . .

I got to know several of the catadores. They posed for photographs based on famous paintings and then came to a studio I constructed near the dump where we created their portraits using garbage. Each photograph was projected onto the floor from high up, on top of a scaffold. We used the projections as outlines and filled in solid areas with old shoes, boxes, cans. Lines were made with bottle caps, and shading was added with dirt.

Everything we used came from the dump. After I took photos of a finished portrait, they took it apart, **RECYCLING** the garbage to make the next one.

Our work was filmed and made into a documentary called **WASTE LAND,** which was nominated for an Academy Award. Tião came with me to the awards ceremony. We didn't win, but it was an **AMAZING JOURNEY** from the garbage dump in Brazil all the way to Hollywood. The portraits have been shown in museums all around the world. Sales of these "Pictures of Garbage" have funded a library and training programs for the catadores.

This is eighteen-year-old Suellen, posed like a Renaissance Madonna with her two children. Working in the dump saved her from a life of drug abuse.

Opposite: *Suellen, Mother and Children,* from the series *Pictures of Garbage,* 2008

This is Carlão posed like Atlas **HOLDING UP THE WORLD.** By making the portraits, Carlão says he learned that sometimes we see ourselves as so small, while people out in the world see us as so big, so beautiful.

Making the portrait *Atlas (Carlão)* in the Jardim Gramacho studio. Opposite: *Atlas (Carlão)*, from the series *Pictures of Garbage*, 2008

I often base my work on **ICONIC** images that you have perhaps seen many times—like the *Mona Lisa* or the *Grande Jatte*. These images are part of our collective **VISUAL MEMORY**.

I have reassembled really popular paintings using jigsaw puzzle pieces. I made my own puzzles, each printed with the same painting but cut differently. In the end, the painting is "solved" . . . but the puzzles remain unsolved.

Above: *La Grande Jatte, after Georges Seurat* from the series *Gordian Puzzles*, 2009. Opposite: *Mona Lisa* (detail) from the series *Gordian Puzzles*, 2009

A LOT OF MY ART IS MADE FROM WHAT PEOPLE TYPICALLY THROW AWAY, LIKE OLD MAGAZINES.

Pictures of Magazines is a series of famous paintings as **COLLAGES,** artworks made out of little bits of torn paper. I photographed the collages and then made huge prints, some as tall as ten feet (3 m). At that size, all the details and the physical **TEXTURE** can overwhelm the scene. What do you focus on—George Washington? Or all the faces and patterns in his cloak?

This work depends on the viewer having an idea of what I am about to show him or her. Art is not something you make alone—you need a viewer, a spectator, an audience. It's a **COLLABORATION**.

Opposite: *Starry Night, after Van Gogh* from the series *Pictures of Magazines 2*, 2012. Under flap: Vincent van Gogh, *The Starry Night*, June 1889. Above: *Washington Crossing the Delaware, after Emanuel Leutze* from the series *Pictures of Magazines 2*, 2012

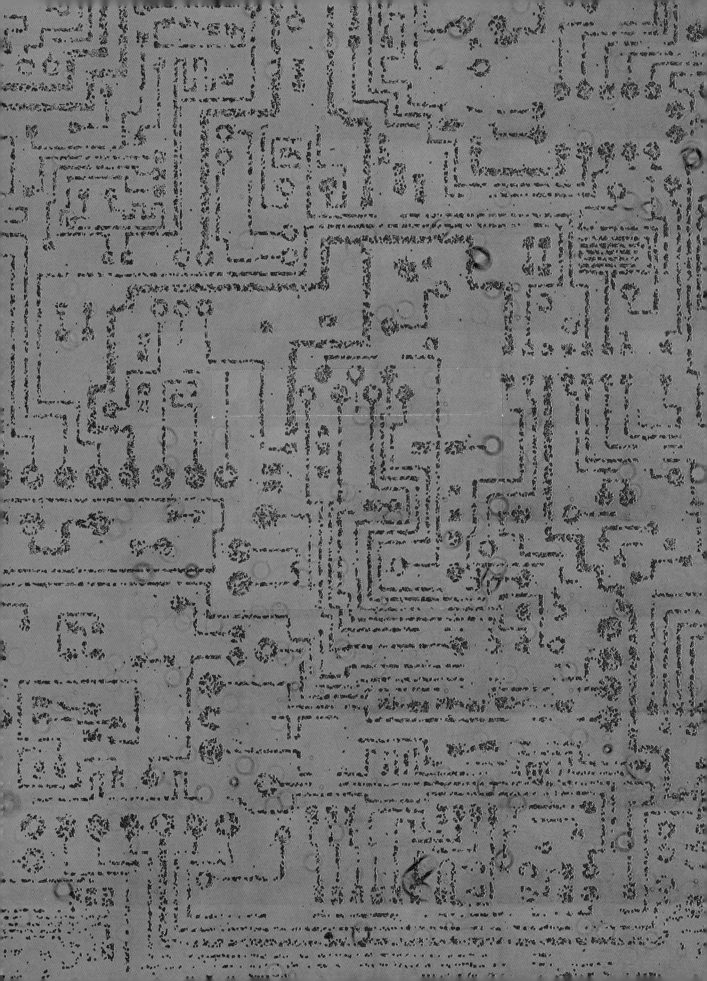

I WANTED TO MAKE IMAGES USING LIVING CELLS.

Another project I worked on at MIT used living cells—bacteria, liver cells, stem cells, cancer cells—to make images. I learned a lot about bacteria. Your body is full of it. We couldn't survive without it. And bacteria is really intelligent—it can communicate by contact. Imagine if by touching you, I could know everything that you know, and you could know everything that I know. That's what bacteria does. Pretty cool, right?

I collaborated with a bioengineer and we invented a technique for making **STENCILS** using collagen (a medium that the cells stick to and grow in) to "paint" patterns.

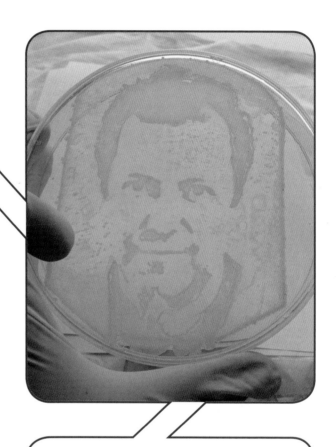

As the cells grew, we took **SCANS** using a microscope. The scans were tiny, about a third of an inch (1 cm) across. One of my first test images was a self-portrait. Then we made patterns, crowd scenes, sports events, traffic jams—even circuit boards.

Opposite: *Motherboard* (detail), from the series *Colonies*, 2014. Above: Vik Muniz's original bacteria portrait

FAMILY ALBUMS TELL A PERSON'S HISTORY.

I have only five photos of myself as a kid. We didn't own a camera. When my aunt visited from the United States, she would bring a camera and take pictures of me. Can you believe I became a photographer? **FAMILY PHOTOS,** printed on paper and saved in an album, were how my generation came to know those who lived before us. That's changing. Now we take LOTS of pictures on our phones—but we seldom print them.

I can find bags of other people's photos for sale on the Internet. That's what I've used to make these collages. They're based on typical family snapshots—baby photos (that's me at two years), weddings, birthdays—but collaged from hundreds of cut-up pictures. If you look closely, you'll see that my baby photo is made from lots and lots of pictures of babies, arranged by shade.

Above: *Wedding,* from the series *Album,* 2014. Opposite: *Vik, 2 Years Old* (detail), from the series *Album,* 2014

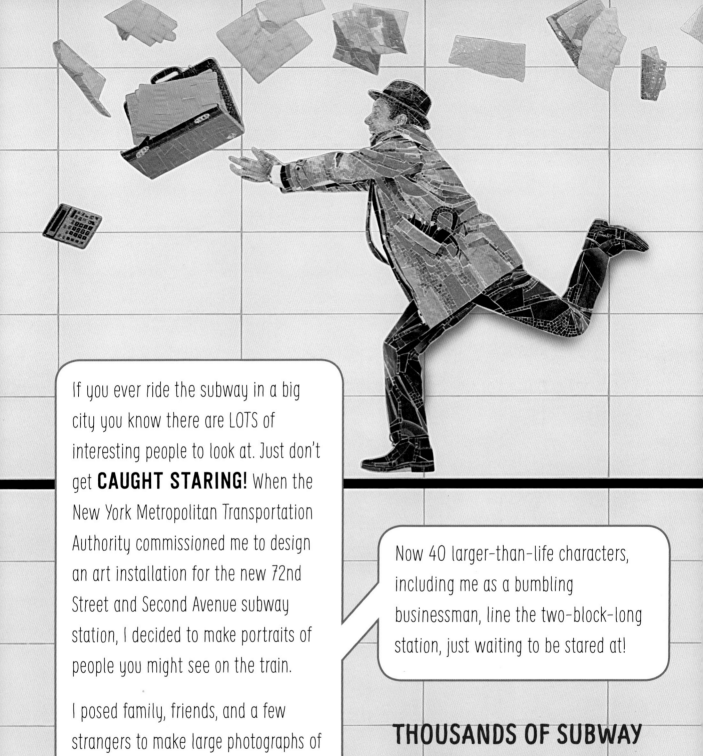

If you ever ride the subway in a big city you know there are LOTS of interesting people to look at. Just don't get **CAUGHT STARING!** When the New York Metropolitan Transportation Authority commissioned me to design an art installation for the new 72nd Street and Second Avenue subway station, I decided to make portraits of people you might see on the train.

I posed family, friends, and a few strangers to make large photographs of some very intriguing commuters. These portraits were then carefully re-created as mosaics by German artisans using colorful **GLASS TILE.**

Now 40 larger-than-life characters, including me as a bumbling businessman, line the two-block-long station, just waiting to be stared at!

THOUSANDS OF SUBWAY RIDERS WILL SEE THESE PORTRAITS EVERY DAY!

ARTISTS ARE VERY BAD AT ANSWERING QUESTIONS,
BUT THEY ARE GOOD AT ASKING THEM.

Lampedusa, floating in the canal at the 56th Venice Biennale, 2015

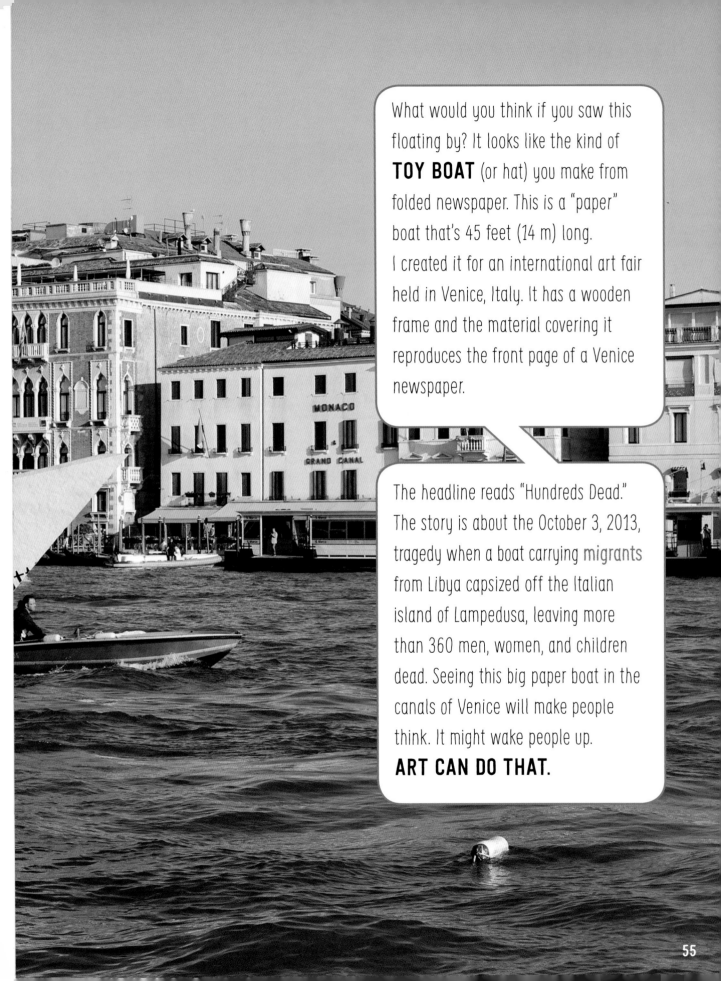

What would you think if you saw this floating by? It looks like the kind of **TOY BOAT** (or hat) you make from folded newspaper. This is a "paper" boat that's 45 feet (14 m) long.

I created it for an international art fair held in Venice, Italy. It has a wooden frame and the material covering it reproduces the front page of a Venice newspaper.

The headline reads "Hundreds Dead." The story is about the October 3, 2013, tragedy when a boat carrying migrants from Libya capsized off the Italian island of Lampedusa, leaving more than 360 men, women, and children dead. Seeing this big paper boat in the canals of Venice will make people think. It might wake people up. **ART CAN DO THAT.**

Age 29 Vik lives in Paris and travels around Europe. While visiting Hungary, Vik encounters guards who demand his visa. He doesn't have one, and when asked to prove he is an artist, he sketches a picture of one of the guards holding a machine gun. "He looked at it," Vik says, "and said, 'Oh, indeed you are an artist! Can you sign it?' After that . . . I could call myself an artist." (1990)

Age 32 Vik returns to New York City from Europe with about one hundred dollars in his pocket. He goes to his studio with a chunk of **plasticene**, a borrowed camera, and an idea. Vik molds the clay to make a small object, then photographs it. "As I didn't have money to buy more material, I had to destroy the first object to make the second—and so on. This exercise took place sixty times, until I ran out of film and patience." *Individuals*, his first solo exhibition, features the photographs alongside empty pedestals representing the missing sculptures. (1992–1993)

Vik's photo of the first of sixty sculptures in the series *Individuals*, 1992–1993

Emerson, from the series *Aftermath*, 1998

Age 34 Vik's series *Sugar Children* is shown at Tricia Collins Contemporary Art in New York City and reviewed in the *New York Times*. A few weeks later Vik is invited to participate in the 1997–1998 New Photography Show at the Museum of Modern Art. (1995)

Age 36 Vik gains recognition for his *Pictures of Chocolate* series, using chocolate syrup to re-create images borrowed from popular culture and then photographing them. He calls this approach the "worst possible illusion." (1997)

Age 37 Invited to participate in the 24th International Biennale in São Paulo, Vik decides to make a series about that cities' homeless children. *Aftermath* features portraits of street kids posed after Old Masters images they choose, which are then re-created using the garbage left on the streets of Rio de Janeiro after Carnaval. (1998)

Age 38 Vik creates *Double Mona Lisa*, after Andy Warhol's appropriation of Da Vinci's muse, which in Muniz's version is portrayed in peanut butter and jelly. (1999)

Age 42 Vik is a guest speaker at the TED Conference in Monterey, California. (2003)

Vik at "play" on his *Rebus* series, 2004

Age 43 Vik creates two new series: *Pictures of Diamonds*, featuring movie stars like Marilyn Monroe made with thousands of the glittery crystals known as "a girl's best friend"; and *Pictures of Caviar*, of villians such as Dracula and Frankenstein's monster made with smelly fish eggs. (2004)

Dracula, from the series *Pictures of Caviar Monsters*, 2004

Age 44 Vik completes the series *Earthworks*, spending three years collaborating with a mining company in Brazil. (2005)

Age 45 Vik founds the Centro Espacial Vik Muniz, an art institute within the Galpão Aplauso school, that 400 students from Rio's comunidades attend each year. (2006)

Age 48 The retrospective *Vik* opens in museums in Rio, São Paulo, and Belo Horizonte, Brazil. The exhibit attracts more than 300,000 visitors. (2009)

Age 49 Vik's collaboration with garbage pickers from the Gramacho landfill in Brazil is made into the documentary *Waste Land*. Directed by Lucy Walker, the film is nominated for an Academy Award and wins many other awards, including the Amnesty International Film Prize and the Sundance Film Festival Audience Award. (2010)

Age 50 Vik participates in "Paper Cranes for Japan," a collaboration with Students Rebuild and the Bezos Family Foundation to benefit victims of the 2011 tsunami. Using thousands of paper cranes folded by children from around the world, Vik creates a mosaic of birds which becomes a poster to benefit the reconstruction effort. (2011)

Age 53 Vik directs (with Juan Rendon) *This Is Not a Ball*, a documentary about how a soccer ball can transform the lives of people around the world. It follows Vik's creative process as he creates an artwork made of 10,000 soccer balls for the 2014 World Cup. (2014)

Ages 55 to 56 Vik builds Escola Vidigal, an art and technology school in Vidigal, one of Rio's hillside comunidades. Scheduled to open in 2017, the school will teach "visual literacy" to local children, ages 4 to 8, offering free preschool and after-school classes in art, design, and technology.

Vik serves as a creative director for the opening ceremony of Rio's 2016 Paralympic Games. His digital artwork, based on the theme "Everybody Has a Heart," lights up Maracanã Stadium when "Brasil," the final puzzle piece, is put in place by the artist.

Perfect Strangers, two blocks of mosaic portraits created from Vik's photographs, are installed at the 72nd Street and 2nd Avenue subway station in New York City. (2016–2017)

Thousands of paper cranes were used to make *Crane* in Vik's Brooklyn studio.

RESOURCES

MUSEUMS

These are some of the many museums around the world you can visit to see Vik Muniz's work in person. To find his work on a gallery or museum's website, type "Vik Muniz" in the search bar.

USA

The Art Institute of Chicago, Chicago, Illinois
www.artic.edu

The Brooklyn Museum, Brooklyn, New York
www.brooklynmuseum.org

Chrysler Museum of Art, Norfolk, Virginia
www.chrysler.org/search/

Cleveland Museum of Contemporary Art, Cleveland, Ohio
www.mocacleveland.org

The Contemporary Museum of Honolulu, Hawaii
www.honolulumuseum.org/11981-spalding_house

The High Museum of Art, Atlanta, Georgia
www.high.org

Los Angeles Museum of Contemporary Art, Los Angeles, California
www.lacma.org

The Menil Collection, Houston, Texas
www.menil.org

The Metropolitan Museum of Art, New York, New York
www.metmuseum.org

Milwaukee Art Museum, Milwaukee, Wisconsin
www.mam.org

The Museum of Fine Arts, Boston, Massachusetts
www.mfa.org

The Museum of Modern Art, New York, New York
www.moma.org

National Gallery of Art, Washington, D.C.
www.nga.gov/content/ngaweb.html

The National Museum of American Art, Smithsonian Institution, Washington, D.C.
www.americanart.si.edu

San Francisco Museum of Modern Art, San Francisco, California
www.sfmoma.org

The Solomon R. Guggenheim Museum, New York, New York
www.guggenheim.org

The Whitney Museum of American Art, New York, New York
www.whitney.org

World

Centre Georges Pompidou, Paris, France
www.centrepompidou.fr/en

Centro Cultural Reina Sofia, Madrid, Spain
www.museoreinasofia.es/en/collection

Daros Latinamerica, Zürich, Switzerland, and Casa Daros, Rio de Janeiro, Brazil
www.daros-latinamerica.net

Gana Art Center, Seoul, Korea
www.ganaart.com

Museu de Arte Moderna de São Paulo, Brazil
www.mam.org.br/en/

The Tate, London, UK
www.tate.org.uk

21st Century Museum of Contemporary Art, Kanazawa, Japan
www.kanazawa21.jp/en/

SELECTED BOOKS

Corrêa do Lago, Pedro, ed. *Everything So Far*. Vik Muniz: Catalog Raisonné, 1987–2015. Rio de Janeiro: Capivara Publishers, 2015. (In Portuguese and English)

McIntosh, DeCourcy E., Andy Grundberg, and Linda Benedict-Jones. *Clayton Days. Picture Stories by Vik Muniz for Very Little Folks*. Pittsburgh: The Frick Art & Historical Center, 2000.

Muniz, Vik. *Reflex: A Vik Muniz Primer*. New York: Aperture Foundation, 2005.

Muniz, Vik, and Éric Mézil. *Vik Muniz: Le Musée imaginaire*. Arles: Actes Sud, 2010. (In French and English)

Muniz, Vik, Diana Murphy, Louisa Stude Sarofim, Matthew Drutt, and Jessica Morgan. *Vik Muniz: Model Pictures*. Houston: The Menil Foundation, 2002.

Ollman, Arthur, and Diana B. Wechsler. *Vik Muniz*. New York: Prestel, 2016.

Soler, Antonio, Fernando Francés, and Juan Uslé. *Vik Muniz Cac Malaga*. Malaga: Contemporary Art Centre in Malaga, 2012. (In Spanish and English)

WEBSITES

Website for *Jelly, Garbage + Toys*:
www.makingpicswithvikmuniz.com

Artist's website: www.vikmuniz.net

Vik Muniz's US gallery:
www.sikkemajenkinsco.com

Vik Muniz's Brazilian gallery:
www.nararoesler.com.br

Links to Vik Muniz works online:
www.artcyclopedia.com/artists/muniz_vik.html

VIDEOS/FILMS

This Is Not a Ball
www.imdb.com/title/tt3776658/

Waste Land
www.wastelandmovie.com/vik-muniz.html

Worst Possible Illusion: The Curiosity Cabinet of Vik Muniz
vimeo.com/ondemand/worstpossibleillusion

TED talk, February 2003
www.ted.com/talks/vik_muniz_makes_art_with_wire_sugar.html

YouTube: Search for Vik Muniz

SOCIAL MEDIA

Like "Vik Muniz Official Page" on Facebook

Instagram: vikmuniz

Twitter: @vikmuniz

GLOSSARY

The numbers in parentheses refer to the page where the term first appears.

abstract Not representing or imitating real life; the opposite of realistic. (29)

action painting A technique and style of abstract painting in which paint is randomly splashed, thrown, or poured on the canvas. It was made famous by the artist Jackson Pollock. (20)

Atlas In Greek mythology Atlas was responsible for holding the weight of the heavens on his shoulders. This was a burden given to him as punishment by Zeus. (42)

bioengineer A person who unites engineering and medicine. Bioengineers work with doctors and researchers to develop equipment and devices to solve clinical problems. (49)

catadore A Portugese word meaning scavenger, or a person who searches through things and collects. (39)

Michelangelo Merisi da **Caravaggio** An Italian painter known for his realistic portrayal of the human condition, and his dramatic use of light (1571–1610). (23)

Paul **Cézanne** A French artist who painted still lifes and landscapes using layered brushstrokes (1839–1906). (30)

circuit board A device which mechanically supports and electrically connects electronic elements. (49)

Chuck **Close** An American artist best known for his large-scale portraits and self-portraits (Born 1940). (29)

collaboration The action of working with someone to produce or create something. (47)

collage From the French verb *coller* (to stick or paste); refers to the process of combining and attaching paper and other objects to a surface using glue. (30)

confetti Small pieces of paper which are usually thrown at parades or parties. (30)

Jean-Baptist-Camille **Corot** A French landscape painter whose style inspired many Impressionists (1796–1875). (14)

documentary A film based on an unusual, interesting real-life event or project. (40)

electron microscope An instrument which magnifies using a beam of electrons, which are particles smaller than an atom. (37)

etch To cut or carve text or a design onto a surface. (37)

focused ion beam A tool used to make microscopic marks. It can etch a line only 50 nanometers wide (a human hair is about 50,000 nanometers wide). (37)

GPS Global Positioning System. A satellite-based navigation system that helps people determine their location. (32)

iconic Relating to or characteristic of a famous person or thing that represents something of importance. (23)

Impressionism A style or movement in painting originating in France in the 1860s, characterized by the shifting effect of light and color. (30)

land sculptures Art forms that are created in nature, using natural materials such as soil, rock, stones, branches, leaves and water. Sculptures are not placed in the landscape, but are made from the land. (32)

light-minute The distance light travels in a vacuum in one minute; approximately 11 million miles. (11)

Madonna In the Christian religion, the Virgin Mary or the mother of Christ. (40)

Jean-Paul **Marat** A political activist, scientist, and journalist who was an advocate for basic human rights for the poor during the French Revolution (1743–1793). (40)

MIT The Massachusetts Institute of Technology located in Cambridge, MA. (37)

migrant A person who travels from one place to another, often to find work. (55)

Claude **Monet** Considered the founder of French Impressionism, he often painted landscapes *en plein air*, or out of doors (1840–1926). (30)

mosaic A picture or decoration made of small, usually colored pieces of inlaid stone, glass or tile. (52)

perspective A technique used to represent three-dimensional objects on a two-dimensional surface in a way that looks natural and realistic. (14)

pixelated In computer graphics, to break up an image into pixels, or an image's smallest possible element. (29)

plasticene A putty-like modeling material made from calcium salts, petroleum jelly, and aliphatic acids that does not dry out. (58)

Jackson **Pollock** An American painter known for his drip painting style (1912–1956). (20)

projected The process of making a picture or movie appear on a surface or screen. (40)

radiating Giving off light or heat in the form of rays or waves. (11)

recognition An acknowledgment of someone or something's existence. (8)

Renaissance The period of time between the 14th and 17th centuries in Europe that bridged the Middle Ages and modern times. The French word means "rebirth." (40)

French Revolution A period of social and political upheaval in France, from 1789 to 1799, when the king was overthrown and a republic established. (40)

Mark **Rothko** An American artist of Russian Jewish descent who made color field paintings (1903–1970). (29)

scaffold A temporary, stable vertical structure that allows people to access heights. (40)

scale The size of an object in relation to another object. (35)

scavenge To search for and collect from discarded waste. (39)

Robert **Smithson** An American artist who was known for his Earthworks sculptures (1938–1973). (32)

stencil A thin sheet of material, like cardboard, plastic, or metal with a pattern cut out of it, used to produce the cut design on the surface below. (49)

Leonardo da **Vinci** An Italian artist, scientist, musician, and inventor regarded as a "Universal Genius" or "Renaissance Man" for his breadth of knowledge and creativity (1452–1519). (23)

visual memory The ability to quickly remember the characteristics of objects, places, animals or people. (44)

LIST OF ILLUSTRATIONS

Works that are shown as details in the book are reproduced here in their entirety.

Vik Muniz artwork © Vik Muniz/Licensed by VAGA, New York, NY

Unless otherwise noted all photographs are by Vik Muniz, and courtesy Vik Muniz Studio.

(Endpapers) *Flowers*, from the series *Colonies*, 2014 (in collaboration with Tal Danino). Digital chromogenic print, dimensions variable

(Page 1) *Cloud Cloud, Manhattan*, from the series *Pictures of Clouds*, 2001. Gelatin silver print, 39 ¾ x 50 in. (101 x 127 cm)

(Page 2–3) *Kyber Pass, Self-portrait as an Oriental, after Rembrandt* (detail), from the series *Pictures of Junk*, 2005. Chromogenic print, 84 x 72 in. (213.3 x 182.9 cm)

(Page 4) Vik with students from PS 8 in Brooklyn, New York, at his studio. Photograph by Joel DeGrand

(Page 5) Photograph of Vik Muniz, circa 1964

Vik Muniz's first drawing, circa 1964

(Page 6) *Clown Skull*, from the series *Relics*, 1989

Cartoon illustrations of Vik Muniz: photographs by Joel DeGrand; drawings by Amanda Freymann

(Page 7) *Tupperware Sarcophage*, 2010

(Page 9) *The Rower*, from the series *Equivalents*, 1993. Platinum palladium print, 10 ½ x 13 in. (26.7 x 33 cm)

(Page 10) *Kitty Cloud*, from the series *Equivalents*, 1993. Platinum palladium print, 10 ½ x 13 in. (26.7 x 33 cm)

(Page 12) *Parcel*, from the series *Pictures of Wire*, 1995. Toned gelatin silver print, 20 x 16 in. (50.8 x 40.6 cm)

Fiat Lux, from the series *Pictures of Wire*, 1995. Toned gelatin silver print, 20 x 16 in. (50.8 x 40.6 cm)

Brooklyn Scene, from the series *Pictures of Wire*, 1994–1995. Toned gelatin silver print, 20 x 16 in. (50.8 x 40.6 cm)

(Page 13) *Homage to Darwin (aka Monkey with Leica)*, from the series *Pictures of Wire*, 1995. Toned gelatin silver print, 20 x 16 in. (50.8 x 40.6 cm)

(Page 14) *16,000 Yards (Le Songeur, after Corot)*, from the series *Pictures of Thread*, 1996. Gelatin silver print, 20 x 24 in. (50.8 x 61 cm)

(Page 17) *Valentina, the Fastest*, from the series *Sugar Children*, 1996. Gelatin silver print, 14 x 11 in. (35.5 x 27.9 cm)

(Page 18) *Ten Ten's Weed Necklace*, from the series *Sugar Children*, 1996. Gelatin silver print, 14 x 11 in. (35.5 x 27.9 cm)

(Page 20) Jackson Pollock, 1950. Photograph by Hans Namuth. Courtesy Center for Creative Photography, University of Arizona © 1991 Hans Namuth Estate

(Page 21) *Action Photo III (after Hans Namuth)*, from the series *Pictures of Chocolate*, 1997. Cibachrome print, 40 x 30 in. (101.6 x 76.2 cm). © Vik Muniz and the Estate of Hans Namuth/VAGA, NY

(Page 22) *Individuals*, from the series *Pictures of Chocolate*, 1998. Cibachrome print, 60 x 48 in. (152.4 x 121.9 cm)

(Page 23) *Double Mona Lisa (Peanut Butter + Jelly)*, from the series *After Warhol*, 1999. Cibachrome print, 47 x 59 in. (119.3 x 149.9 cm)

Medusa Marinara, 1999. Cibachrome print, diam. 12 in. (30.5 cm)

Michelangelo Merisi da Caravaggio (1571–1610), Medusa, painted on a leather jousting shield, c. 1596–98. Oil on canvas on poplar shutter (post restoration). Galleria degli Uffizi, Florence, Italy / Bridgeman Images

(Page 24) Unidentified photographer, portrait of Pvt. Edwin Francis Jemison, 2nd Louisiana Regiment, C.S.A. Library of Congress, Prints & Photographs Division, Civil War Photographs, [reproduction number, LC-B8184-10037]

(Page 25) *Toy Soldier*, from the series *Monads*, 2003. Chromogenic print, 92 x 72 in. (233.7 x 182.9 cm)

(Pages 26–27) *Self Portrait (I Am Too Sad to Tell You, after Bas Jan Ader)*, from the series *Rebus*, 2003. Chromogenic print, 89 x 70 ¾ in. (226 x 180 cm)

(Page 28) *Chuck*, from the series *Pictures of Color*, 2001. Chromogenic print, 72 x 98 ½ in. (183 x 250 cm)

(Page 29) *After Mark Rothko*, from the series *Pictures of Color*, 2001. Chromogenic print, 98 x 70 ⅞ in. (249 x 180 cm)

(Page 30) *Irises after Van Gogh*, from the series *Pictures of Magazines*, 2004. Chromogenic print, 95 ¼ x 71 ⅝ in. (242 x 182 cm)

(Page 31) *Still Life with Apples after Cézanne*, from the series *Pictures of Magazines*, 2004. Chromogenic print, 72 x 97 ⅝ in. (183 x 248 cm)

Paul Cézanne (1839–1906), *Still Life with Apples*, c. 1890. Oil on canvas. State Hermitage Museum, St. Petersburg, Russia / Bridgeman Images

(Page 32) *Brooklyn, New York (Spiral Jetty, after Robert Smithson)*, 1979. 19 ⅝ x 30 in. (50 x 76 cm)

Vik working on *Brooklyn, New York*

(Page 33) *Scissors*, from the series *Earthworks*, 2002. Toned gelatin silver print, 20 x 24 in. (50.8 x 61 cm)

(Page 34) *Outlet (Fabrica, Iron Mine)*, from the series *Earthworks*, 2005. Toned gelatin silver print, 20 x 24 in. (50.8 x 61 cm)

(Page 35) *Sock*, from the series *Pictures of Earthworks*, 2002. Toned gelatin silver print, 20 x 24 in. (50.8 x 61 cm)

Glasses, from the series *Pictures of Earthworks*, 2002. Toned gelatin silver print, 20 x 24 in. (50.8 x 61 cm)

Footsteps (João Pereira, Iron Mine), from the series *Earthworks*, 2005. Toned gelatin silver print, 20 x 24 in. (50.8 x 61 cm)

Female (João Pereira, Iron Mine), from the series *Earthworks*, 2005. Toned gelatin silver print, 20 x 24 in. (50.8 x 61 cm)

(Page 36) *Sandcastle #3*, from the series *Sandcastles*, 2013 (in collaboration with Marcelo Coelho). Digital chromogenic print, 71 x 84 ½ in. (180.3 x 214.6 cm)

(Page 37) Vik with the FIB machine at MIT

Sandcastle #1, from the series *Sandcastles*, 2013 (in collaboration with Marcelo Coelho). Digital chromogenic print, dimensions variable

Sandcastle #10, from the series *Sandcastles*, 2014. Digital chromogenic print, 70 ⅞ x 86 ⅝ in. (180 x 220 cm)

(Pages 38–39) Mountains of garbage at the Jardim Gramacho landfill, 2006

(Page 40) Tião, posing as Jean-Paul Marat, 2008

Jacques Louis David (1748–1825). *The Death of Marat*, 1793. Oil on canvas. Musees Royaux des Beaux-Arts de Belgique, Brussels, Belgium / Bridgeman Images

Marat (Sebastião), from the series *Pictures of Garbage*, 2008. Digital chromogenic print, 30 x 24 in. (76.2 x 61 cm)

Irma, posing as Bearer, 2008

Statue of an Offering Bearer (detail). Egyptian; Thebes, Southern Asasif, c. 1981–1975 BCE. Wood, gesso, paint, 44 ⅛ x 6 ½ x 18 ⁵⁄₁₆ in. (112 x 16.5 x 46.5 cm). © The Metropolitan Museum of Art. Image source: Art Resource NY

Irma, The Bearer, from the series *Pictures of Garbage*, 2008. Chromogenic print, 30 x 24 in. (76.2 x 61 cm)

(Page 41) *Suellen, Mother and Children*, from the series *Pictures of Garbage*, 2008. Chromogenic print, 30 x 24 in. (76.2 x 61 cm)

(Page 42) Making the portrait *Atlas (Carlão)* in the Jardim Gramacho studio, 2008

Page 40

(Page 43) *Atlas (Carlão)*, from the series *Pictures of Garbage*, 2008. Digital chromogenic print, 30 x 24 in. (76.2 x 61 cm)

(Page 44) *La Grande Jatte, after Georges Seurat*, from the series *Gordian Puzzles*, 2009. Digital chromogenic print, 92 x 70 ⅞ in. (233.7 x 180 cm)

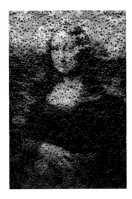

(Page 45) *Mona Lisa*, from the series *Gordian Puzzles*, 2009. Digital chromogenic print, 97 x 65 in. (246.4 x 165 cm)

(Page 46) *Starry Night, after Van Gogh*, from the series *Pictures of Magazines 2*, 2012. Digital chromogenic print, 70 ⅞ x 89 in. (180 x 226 cm)

Vincent van Gogh (1853–90), *The Starry Night*, June 1889. Oil on canvas. Museum of Modern Art, New York, USA / Bridgeman Images

(Page 47) *Washington Crossing the Delaware, after Emanuel Leutze*, from the series *Pictures of Magazines 2*, 2012. Digital chromogenic print, 60 x 108 ¼ in. (152.4 x 275 cm)

(Page 48) *Motherboard*, from the series *Colonies*, 2014 (in collaboration with Tal Danino). Digital chromogenic print, 70 ⅞ x 90 ½ in. (180 x 230 cm)

(Page 49) Bacteria portrait of Vik Muniz (in collaboration with Tal Danino)

(Page 50) *Wedding*, from the series *Album*, 2014. Digital chromogenic print, 89 x 71 in. (226 x 180.3 cm)

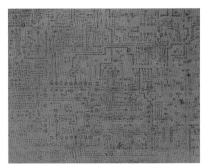

Page 48

(Page 51) *Vik, 2 Years Old*, from the series *Album*, 2014. Digital chromogenic print, 99 ½ x 71 in. (252.7 x 180.3 cm)

(Pages 52–53) *Perfect Strangers* (2016) © Vik Muniz, NYC Transit 2nd Avenue Subway–72 Street Station. Commissioned by MTA Arts & Design. Images courtesy of MTA Arts & Design and Franz Mayer of Munich

Work in progress at Franz Mayer of Munich. Image by Franz Mayer of Munich. Used with permission

(Pages 54–55) *Lampedusa*, floating in the canal at the 56th Venice Biennale, 2015

(Page 57) Peter Paul Rubens (1577–1640). *A Child's Head* (*Portrait of Clara Serena Rubens*), c. 1616. Oil on canvas on wood panel. © 2017 LIECHTENSTEIN, The Princely Collections, Vaduz-Vienna / Scala, Florence / Art Resource NY

Page 51

(Page 58) *Emerson*, from the series *Aftermath*, 1998. Cibachrome print, 59 ⅞ x 47 ⅝ in. (152 x 121 cm)

Dracula, from the series *Pictures of Caviar Monsters*, 2004

(Page 59) *Crane*, 2011. 71 x 88 ¾ in. (180.3 x 225.3 cm)

This Is Not A Ball. Photograph courtesy Videocine

2016 Paralympic Opening ceremony. Photographs courtesy Rio 2016 Paralympic Games

Acknowledgments

This book is based on a studio visit by twelve 3rd grade students from PS 8 in Brooklyn, New York, who visited Vik Muniz with their teachers. Thank you to the young artists—Jasmia Davis, Mikiara Davis, Sam Elliot, Warner Gephardt, Leonardo Gerunda, Faith Jones, Luena Leitao, Harris Levnjak, Hadley Lewis, Lola Raman-Middleton, Hoddy Smith, and Lucian Terhorst—for your great questions. And a big thank-you to teaching artist Jenny Bevill and classroom teachers Ashley Coates and Sjene Kendrick.

A huge thank-you to Erika Benincasa, studio manager for Vik Muniz, and to Dillon DeWaters and Paty Lopez for assisting us at every turn.

Many thanks to Phyllis B. Dooney, Nacho Corbella, and Joel DeGrand for the videography, audio, and photography of the studio visit.

We are grateful to Howard Reeves, our editor at Abrams and a trusted colleague and friend, for supporting us along this journey. Many thanks to the team at Abrams—Orlando Dos Reis, Alison Gervais, Chad W. Beckerman, James Armstrong, and Masha Gunic.

Thanks to Ernie, Joel, and Scott for your love and support.

Vik Muniz would like to thank his wife, Malu, and his children, Dora, Mina, Francesco, and Gaspar.

We thank Vik for enthusiastically collaborating on this project. His ability to make meaning and magic happen whether working with diamonds or garbage is contagious. We hope his work will inspire artists of all ages to embrace the importance of play, and to make art from anything and everything.

—JES, AWF + AKD

Index

Cataloging-in-Publication Data has been applied for and may be obtained from the Library of Congress.

ISBN 978-1-4197-2575-3

© 2017 Glue + Paper Workshop, LLC

Vik Muniz artwork © Vik Muniz/Licensed by VAGA, New York, NY

All other art credits see pages 62–63.

Front cover: Double Mona Lisa (Peanut Butter + Jelly) (detail), from the series After Warhol, 1999. Cibachrome print, 47 x 59 in. (119.3 x 149.9 cm)

A Glue + Paper Workshop Book for Kids created by Joan Sommers and Amanda Freymann, with Ascha Drake. www.glueandpaper.com

Cover and interior design: Joan Sommers

Printed and bound in China

10 9 8 7 6 5 4 3 2 1

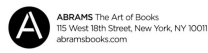

ABRAMS The Art of Books
115 West 18th Street, New York, NY 10011
abramsbooks.com